4-26-95

D0388706

*Dear Cindy —*
*May you know in your heart, that*

# "**Trouble Don't Last Always**"
## Soul Prayers

Diana L. Hayes

*Much love &*
*"Prayers always"*

*Paula Palmateer*

*A Liturgical Press Book*

 THE LITURGICAL PRESS
Collegeville, Minnesota

Cover design by Greg Becker.

| 1 | 2 | 3 | 4 | 5 | 6 | 7 | 8 |
|---|---|---|---|---|---|---|---|

**Library of Congress Cataloging-in-Publication Data**

Hayes, Diana L.
    Trouble don't last always : soul prayers / Diana L. Hayes.
        p.    cm.
    Includes bibliographical references.
    ISBN 0-8146-2297-6
    1. Hayes, Diana L.  2. Afro-American Catholics—Biography.
3. Afro-American theologians—Biography.  4. Rheumatoid arthritis-
-Patients—Biography.  5. Afro-Americans—Music—Meditations.
6. Suffering—Religious aspects—Christianity—Meditations.
I. Title.
BX4705.H344A3   1995
282'.092—dc20
  [B]                              94-48429
                                             CIP

## Dedication

This book is dedicated to all who, like
me, struggle daily with a chronic illness,
but it is meant for all who have found
themselves, at times, "soul-sick and weary"
in the hope that these prayers of my soul may
give you the inspiration to "keep on keepin'
on."

# Contents

# Introduction
## Trouble Don't Last Always

Reality for Blacks in the U.S. has always been one of
seeming paradox. "Trouble" always seems to be in our
way, regardless of the form it takes, from forced migra-
tion, slavery, second-class citizenship, to the constant
enervating struggle with proponents of racism and the
lack of opportunity for education, decent health treatment, and a life of dignity and happiness. Yet through
it all, or, perhaps it can be said, because of it all, we have
been a people with our eyes "fixed" on God; a people
for whom "trouble don't last always."

> Trouble in my way,
> I have to cry sometimes.
> Trouble in my way,
> I have to cry sometimes.

The spirituals, blues, and other forms of Black music
that have emerged in the U.S. are the "soul prayers" of
Black Americans. Forbidden to read or write, illiterate
slaves wrote their transforming and liberating theologies
in the books of their souls and transcribed them in the
depths of their hearts, then passed them on, literally, from
mouth to mouth, from ear to ear, down through the
generations.

1

This music—once thought to be based on hopes for an eventual, peaceful death and a pleasant life afterwards in a "land flowing with milk and honey" where me and you and "all God's children" would have shoes, warm clothes, and all of the other needful things missing from a life filled with harshness and want—can be seen to be songs not of defeat or acquiescence, but of a constant, enduring, burning faith in a God who loves, a God who liberates, a God who acts in history, in the here-and-now of everyday life, to bring about relief from pain, hunger, and oppression.

> I lay awake at night
> But that's alright
> I know my Jesus will fix it
> After a while.

My own life has enabled me to follow, at times unwillingly, the struggles of my people and to experience the pain of being "different" in too many ways to make life in this world, with its stress on conformity, an unvarnished blessing.

I grew up the second child in a family of four girls. From the very beginning of my life, I was labeled "different" by a world that did not understand the thirst, the hunger for knowledge that resided within me. Having somehow learned to read by the time I was three years old, I was never satisfied with the "arbitrary" restrictions I felt placed on my life by my family's poverty or the fact that I was both Black and female at a time when being either or both was seen as of little importance or value.

Yet I persevered in my efforts to be educated, "devouring" all of the books in our neighborhood branch library by the time I was ten years old, then walking miles to the downtown library to tap into that seemingly endless source of literary wealth. I loved classical music as well, an interest that brought consternation to my sisters who were used to listening to rhythm and blues. I was deeply moved by the spirituals and blues and by the soulful strains of jazz, again, tastes no one else in my family seemed to have.

I loved poetry of all kinds, by writers of all races. By the time I finished high school, I had read the Bible in its entirety in at least four or five different versions, from the King James (in which I, a child of the African Methodist Episcopal Zion Church, had been brought up) to the New English, the International, the Revised Standard, and even the Living Bible.

I wanted to know more than many believed was good for me—a Black girlchild destined only to marry and have children and no more in life.

My growing up years were ones split between bursts of athletic energy—as I spent most of my time with the boys in my neighborhood playing every sport available to us as vigorously as I could—and times of reflective quiet spent in bed reading while I recuperated from one illness or another.

Paradoxically, it was those quiet times which always gave me the strength to go back out into the world again. God has always seemed to come to me in those days of pain-filled darkness and disillusionment, to hold my hand, to counsel me, to prepare me to go forth renewed in spirit and body.

I left the AMEZion Church at fifteen years of age, against the wishes of my parents, but eventually with their somewhat reluctant acknowledgement (and heart-felt prayer) that I would one day return. I did return to the Church in my thirty-second year of life, but it was a different one—the Roman Catholic Church—that opened its arms to me after seventeen years of a search I was unaware I had embarked upon.

During those seventeen years most of my time was spent in two ways, first furthering my education as I went from high school to college to law school and law practice, then back for further studies on the master's level, before finding myself as a lawyer for New York State in Albany. Second, it was spent in the mountains and forests of the many state and national parks around the Washington, D.C., and Albany areas, with occasional forays overseas.

It was especially on those weekends spent, not in a sterile, stone church, but in the living, spirit-filled wooden cathedrals of God's creation that my faith was constantly reaffirmed and strengthened. I never lost sight of God's "all-powerful hand" during those seventeen years of separation from any institutional form of church; rather, that hand seemed more apparent than ever, leading and guiding me on.

I became a Roman Catholic for one reason only, in response to what I believed then, and still believe today, to be a direct and insistent call from God. It was not a call that initially I wanted to answer because I knew it would totally disrupt the comfortable life I had become accustomed to. But it was a call that I could neither ignore nor deny and still remain the person I thought I was.

To my consternation—and that of my family and friends—I, an independent (some would say "uppity") Black woman, found God in the Roman Catholic Church, a Church not known particularly for its welcoming attitude toward either Blacks or women. Yet I felt nurtured, loved, and desired by God within that Church and by the people I was led to who helped me to become a part of that Church, most, but not all, of whom were themselves Roman Catholics.

It is here, during the process of my conversion to Catholicism and my return to graduate school to undertake the study of theology, that my life began, for me, to truly reflect the "soul-prayers" expressed in Black religious music. For no sooner had I begun the study of the Catholic faith than I was stricken with a degenerative disease in my knees that forced me to leave my beloved woods behind and learn the lesson that God is truly every-where, supporting us on every leaning side.

The disease, chondromallatia, reduced me, in a few short months, to a pain-filled, grieving, angry woman, bed-ridden and questioning both her own sanity and that of God. Why become a Catholic if I will never be able to kneel in Church, thus making me, as it seemed then at that sensitive stage of conversion, an even more obvi-ous misfit in a parish where there were only four other Blacks, a single mother with her three sons.

I wrestled with God on my bed of pain as I do still today. I do not and cannot take God's love simply for granted, but must thrash it out until I can understand, for myself, where I am being led. I argue and shout and listen and pray and question and doubt and finally ac-quiesce only to move further down the path to another fork in the road where the struggle begins yet anew.

Since that fateful day in September of 1979 when, while at work, first one, and then the other, knee sud-denly swelled up and began to throb unbearably, I have not spent a day of my life without some form of pain, great or small, reminding me of my human frailty and, by extension, of the frailty of others.

Although in time I was able to move beyond braces and crutches to a cane, and eventually to the freedom of walking unassisted once again, I have been made very much aware since that day of God's activity in my own life—an activity which, at times, has seemed paradoxical and unintelligible, but which, in time, has enabled me to take a further step along the path toward home. Over the past fifteen years since my confirmation into the Roman Catholic Church in 1979, I have undergone major surgery four times, struggled through long periods of re-cuperation, and, since 1987, dealt with the reality of a chronic illness, rheumatoid arthritis, which I have finally realized and slowly begun to accept will never go away.

Yet during those same fifteen years, I have successfully completed the pontifical program in theology, beginning at the Catholic University of America and finishing with a Ph.D. in Religious Studies, as well as the Doctor of Sacred Theology (S.T.D.) degree from the Catholic University of Louvain, Belgium. I have become an associate, tenured professor at Georgetown University and have discovered the end toward which all of those years of reading had been preparing me: the life of a scholar and teacher, professions equally important to me.

I believe I have learned, because of my own struggles, how to see, hear, and feel the struggles of others, voiced and unvoiced. This has led me to explore theology and the role of the Christian Churches in the U.S. in a new and challenging way—from the bottom up. I know what it is like to be poor, to be discriminated against because of my poverty, my race, my gender, and my disabilities. These many years of struggle and pain, which continue to this day, have forged me in the fiery furnace of God's love. I firmly believe that I have been sent to be of service to those who, unlike myself, have not yet found their voices and been awakened to the graced but burdensome knowledge that, as children of a loving God, they are sent not to suffer, but to live a life free from oppression.

The "soul-prayers" that make up this brief but, for me, all encompassing work are those that helped carry me over the rock-strewn and rough places of my life over the past years. Although I am, for the most part, referring in them to my on-going battle with rheumatoid arthritis, in actuality these prayers of my heart reflect all of the years of my journeying toward communion with God, a God whom I know loves and cherishes me.

This story is not over and, hopefully, will not be over for many years to come. But my growth from anger and despair to acceptance and perseverance is one that I believe is repeated in the lives of many around me who struggle daily with pain, whether its form is physical, mental, or spiritual. And, as I have found, where one form exists, the others are usually close behind.

It is not over. The anger still bubbles to the surface at times; the despair creeps in unannounced and sideswipes me leaving me befuddled and confused, but the knowledge that through it all God is steadfastly present in my life sustains and strengthens me.

My life, a seeming paradox of contradictions and odd twists and turns, has truly been one where troubles of many different forms have always been in my way. Yet I know now, deep within me, that "trouble don't last always." God is not through with me yet.

# Yet Do I Marvel [1]

My life has been a journey of fits and starts, flowing smoothly at times, sluggishly at others, sometimes barely getting anywhere at all, at other times getting "there" much too fast. . . . Part of that journey, especially for the last fifteen years, I have shared with another, the presence of constant pain.

I am a theologian, my head is full of ideas, thoughts, sounds, and words eager to leap forth from my mind through my fingers onto the written page. Yet, the closer I have come to fulfilling what I believe to be my vocation—to be a voice for the voiceless, to be one who stands up for those unable or afraid to stand up for themselves—the more difficult it has become, physically, to do so.

I am a writer whose hands swell up and whose fingers become useless after only a few sentences have been written. Yet I grit my teeth and continue to write, watching the words—so clear and stark in my mind—become scrambled and illegible on the pieces of paper on which I am trying to write.

I am a Roman Catholic who has never kneeled in humble submission before the figure of Christ because at the same time that I was in the process of conversion to the Catholic faith, I was also in the process of losing

---

[1] The title is from the poem by Harlem Renaissance poet Countee Cullen.

the ability to run, to walk, to stand, and even to kneel.

And "yet do I marvel" because, despite all of this, the urge to write, that creative fire, still burns within me, and apparently nothing and no one can quench it. So I have learned to work around and through the pain, rewarding myself with hot baths and heating pads after a certain amount of work has been achieved.

I developed rheumatoid arthritis in the last year of my doctoral work at the Catholic University of Louvain in Belgium in 1987. I believe that, although it is thought to be a genetically inherited disease, it was probably also brought on by the stress of completing my dissertation and living in a foreign country with a cold, damp climate. My doctor and I had a running joke as to which would be "finished" first, the dissertation or me, and I almost won (or lost?). The disease did not slowly creep into my life, but burst upon me with a blaze of pain and paralytic fury that only a massive assault of medical treatment could slow down. Even today, when discussing my condition with my new doctor, I feel as if I am describing a war taking place within the confines, the battleground, of my body. We speak of "flare-ups" and "hot-spots" and "assaults" on various joints as if we were anchors on a network news show discussing the latest country under siege. It is a guerrilla war—waged by a silent but vicious enemy who has vowed to succeed against all odds, who attacks at odd times, never in the same place, popping out here or there to slow down or stiffen or swell up or immobilize one part or another of my body.

"Yet do I marvel"—for through it all, even despite it all, I still struggle to write, for the voices within me will not be silenced. It is an exhausting battle—I never know from one day to the next whether I will be able to rise to meet the dawn or will have to greet it lying flat on my back or sitting up somewhere in between. Making plans can become meaningless and frustrating when the legs you believed would carry you out for a walk on a sunny day decide they would prefer not to carry any weight at all today—thank you anyway. It is frustrating, yet I do not—I cannot—give up. The struggle is within me and all around me, yet still I fight to put the words down that speak to me and, hopefully, to others—words of freedom, of liberation, of faith in a God who loves, a God who frees, a God who "makes a way out of no way."

There are times when I do not understand why I have this disease. There are times when I feel like giving up—giving in to the pain and simply letting it take over not just my body, but my mind as well. But I find I cannot do that. For I am constantly and persistently called out of myself by those around me who seem to feel that my words bring hope into their lives. They do not realize how much their response brings hope back into mine.

And so I marvel at this curious thing, "that God would make a poet black, and bid [her] sing!"[2] I, a Black woman, at times completely overpowered by this disease that has taken up residence within me, am bidden over and over by this God, in whom I have put all of my trust, to sing. And so I sing, and in the singing I too am free.

So I share with you the prayers of my soul not in bitterness or in defeat, but in acknowledgement of the importance of prayer and God's love in my life. I also hope that my words, written in and about suffering, may ease your own.

Most of these pieces were written during the time from dusk to dawn when, because of pain or malaise caused by my disease or due to the effects of the many different medicines I take to curb it, I was unable to sleep. Many times I found peace in those still hushed hours; at other times, only anger and frustration. All of these feel-

---

[2] Countee Cullen, "Yet Do I Marvel," *My Soul's High Song: The Collected Writings of Countee Cullen* (New York: Anchor Books, 1991) 79.

ings fueled this collection of essays I have entitled "soul prayers" because I do believe that they come from the very depths of my soul.

# *In the Garden*

I come to the garden alone,
While the dew is still on the roses;
And the voice I hear, falling on my ear,
The Son of God discloses.

And He walks with me,
And He talks with me,
And He tells me I am His own,
And the joy we share as we tarry there,
None other has ever known. (Refrain)

He speaks, and the sound of His voice
Is so sweet the birds hush their singing;
And the melody that He gave to me
Within my heart is ringing.

I'd stay in the garden with Him
Though the night around me be falling;
But He bids me go thru the voice of woe,
His voice to me is calling.[1]

When I was young, waiting impatiently in the pews
of St. Luke AMEZion Church for Sunday services to end,
there was always one song sung by the Cathedral Choir
that could still my childish restlessness and bring me a
sense of peace. The song would awaken a yearning within
me that, at the time, I did not understand. The words

[1] Text: C. Austin Miles, 1868–1946.

and melody of this song are one of my earliest memories, and whenever I hear it sung today it brings forth fond memories of my uncle "Rev's" church, of me and my sisters lined up and moving out the door to Sunday School on so many Sunday mornings, of a sense of coolness on even the hottest of days, of the men and women of St. Luke, both the old and the new church, who served as surrogate parents—at times to our frustration—ensuring that we children received the love and discipline that we needed to grow up and out into the world.

Today, in times of deep despair, the faint strains of that song often come back to me, weaving a web of peace and comfort, reminding me of a time when all was well with my life.

> I come to the garden alone,
> While the dew is still on the roses;
> And the voice I hear, falling on my ear,
> The Son of God discloses.

It is an old-fashioned song that is not heard often today. It is easy to sing and to remember and I remember it still, often in the voice of my grandmother as she played on her old upright, singing softly while we played around her on those hot summer days in Chattanooga, Tennessee.

> And He walks with me,
> And He talks with me,
> And He tells me I am His own,
> And the joy we share as we tarry there,
> None other has ever known.

It is a song of love, a song of caring, a song that gives a sense of belonging, of being welcomed and wanted, feelings so many today, especially our children, seem never to have experienced.

So many seem to feel God's love has to be bargained for or bought at a high price, that you have to do or be something grand or perfect in order to "earn" God's love, but the words of this song and the understanding behind it give the lie to those beliefs. Instead, it reveals that God's love is available to all if one just believes; if one has the faith of a trusting, innocent, and vulnerable child.

I always imagined myself and Jesus walking in the garden like old friends, laughing and chatting, pausing to look at the beauty of the flowers, then setting forth once again. We did not talk of serious things, of sin or death, evil or punishment, but of little things, my hopes and dreams for the future, my love of life, his love for me and all of creation. I realize now that this song, in many ways, shaped my understanding of God and my faith in God.

To me, God has always been someone who listened—like my grandfather did while we sat in his garden—who was patient with me, who spent time with me and let me rattle on about anything and everything that was on my mind and in my heart. God is a father and a mother to me, but also a big brother, something I never had, who did not make fun of my love of learning, of my hunger for books, of my thirst for exploring new worlds and meeting new people, of the way I talked or of my "tomboyishness."

Later in life, when I left the AMEZion Church with the impatience and frustration of youth looking for I knew not what elsewhere, that same God was still with me, walking alongside me in the mountains, floating down the rivers, skiing down the trails. I had left the institutional form of the Church but I was still a part of the Body of Christ and Christ was still a part of me. His message, his words, his love have shaped me and formed me and set me on the path that brought me home to the Roman Catholic Church where I am today.

> He speaks, and the sound of His voice
> Is so sweet the birds hush their singing;

And the melody that He gave to me
Within my heart is ringing.

I carry that melody with me wherever I go and I attempt to sing it, in various ways, for others. The melody
bursts forth in my writing about freedom, a freedom
promised by God to all of God's creation. Hopefully, it
radiates from me in my lectures and workshops on a liberating theology, revealing to my students the responsibility
that we all share, as co-partners in creation, in the effort
to bring about a better world for all. It leaps from my
very being in my efforts to witness to Christ in my own
life, to overcome the hurdles and obstacles in my path
brought about by disease—both the physical disease with
which I have been blessed/cursed and the psychological
and societal diseases of racism, sexism, and classism that
others project upon me.

I'd stay in the garden with Him
Though the night around me be falling;
But He bids me go thru the voice of woe,
His voice to me is calling.

The temptation for me, for the apostles, for all of us,
is to stay with Jesus, secure in his love for us and safe
from the temptations and seductions of the world. But
he calls us forth, challenging us to go out into the world
and work toward its redemption. It is a frightening challenge at times, but a necessary one. For we are called as
disciples, sent forth to proclaim the good news. We cannot be apostles in the warmth and security of the garden, but must leave it over and over again in order to
one day return for good by making a garden of all the
world.

The foundation that I received in my Church and in
my home has enabled me to go forth into the world, even
though it is too often a harsh and frightening one. I go

because I know I do not walk alone but have a constant, loving companion who, in the stillness of my lonely, pain-filled nights, still walks and talks with me and reminds me, constantly, that I am his own.

I thank you, Lord, for choosing me
Even though there are times
    when I may seem less than grateful.
I have learned to love because you love,
    I have learned to care because you care,
I have learned to try to live my life in service to others
    because you lived and died in service to all.
Thank you, Lord, for your gift of life, of love, of belonging.
Show me the way to pass on your gifts to others
    so that they too may share in the joys of your
        garden,
The garden of Life.

# I Know What the Caged Bird Feels

### Sympathy[1]

I know what the caged bird feels, alas!
When the sun is bright on the upland slopes;
When the wind stirs soft through the springing grass
And the river flows like a stream of glass;
When the first bird sings and the first bud opes,
And the faint perfume from its chalice steals—
I know what the caged bird feels!

I know why the caged bird beats his wing
Till its blood is red on the cruel bars:
For he must fly back to his perch and cling
When he fain would be on the bough a-swing:
And a pain still throbs in the old, old scars
And they pulse again with a keener sting—
I know why he beats his wing!

I know why the caged bird sings, ah me,
When his wing is bruised and his bosom sore—
When he beats his bars and would be free;
It is not a carol of joy or glee,
But a prayer that he sends from his heart's deep core,
But a plea, that upward to Heaven he flings—
I know why the caged bird sings!

—Paul Laurence Dunbar

[1] *The Poetry of Black America: An Anthology of the 20th Century,* ed. Arnold Adolf (New York and San Francisco: Harper & Row) 8.

Yes, "I know what the caged bird feels." The words of Paul Laurence Dunbar's poignant poem sound in my ears and in the corners of my mind almost constantly now. Truly, "I know what the caged bird feels, alas!"

At first, when I was told that the reason for my strange aches and pains, for the stiffness in my hands and knees, was rheumatoid arthritis, I simply took it in stride, or so I thought. Another battle to overcome. My life, it seems, has been plagued (or, perhaps, blessed) with various battles that had to be fought one by one. As a Black woman in the U.S., I am used to fighting battles. But this one was different.

I could not ignore it because if I did I found myself slowly freezing into an immovable statue. I could not bargain with it: "Okay, I'll stay in bed all of today but tomorrow I'm going hiking." This disease was sneaky; it did not—and still does not—play fair. It is insidious and pervasive; it has infiltrated every part of my being, every one of my joints, clamoring for attention, seeking to be heard and dealt with. It is not willing to be put aside until I am able to deal with it in my own time. It has a rhythm of its own which, as yet, I cannot accustom myself to.

I cannot run away from it because I can no longer run. In the past five years since rheumatoid arthritis began its pernicious assault on my body, I have become a shadow of the person I was. Once a year-round athlete, proficient in too many sports to name and loving the strength and vigor of my body, now I find myself exhausted after a two-block walk, unable to keep up with my own mother who is almost thirty years older than me. I am confined, restrained by the body that once took me everywhere and with which I did so much. I am now its captive rather than its master.

And so I mourn, like the caged bird, at the change of seasons, at the coming of spring when I would be the first on the hills seeking out the new-budding azaleas and rhododendrons. I grieve over the fall with its flamboyant burst of colors running riot in woods where I no longer can easily walk. I wander lost through the winters and springs without my usual bearings, my senses heightened but my responses dulled.

But as I grieve, I cannot help thinking of others who are also trapped, not like myself in a cage made by the body, but in the cages made by others—the cages of the ghettos and barrios, the barred rooms of poverty and the locked doors of despair. And I wonder; I wonder why I have been afflicted in this way. Is it not burden enough, at times, to be both Black and female? Why have others, like myself, been afflicted with poverty or illness or illiteracy?

Is it the will of God? No, for my God is a good and loving God who does not inflict pain and suffering for the hell of it. Is it my fault? No, for I, and these others, have committed no sin or evil for which we should be punished. God does not punish, he[2] is a God of forgiveness and freedom. It is not a crime to be poor or homeless or Black or a woman. The blame, if blame there is, must be laid at the doors of a society that finds fault with those seen as "handicapped" because of their race, gender, age, or physical condition. However, those of us so "afflicted" are left with the responsibility, the necessity, of overcoming the limitations upon us, whether real or imposed, and of working, as best we can, to become the persons we are capable of being, by overcoming the pain, by obtaining the skills necessary to rise out of poverty, by taking charge of our own lives, by allowing

[2] Throughout this text, I use "he" for God. This is because, for me, God has always been male, not in any patriarchal or oppressive sense, but in the sense of God as loving father and caring brother. I also see God as female and as spirit (without gender). But in these soul prayers, I am speaking to, with, and about God in my own understanding. The reader is free to use whatever language about God he or she prefers.

no one to "turn us around." And it is God, my faith in him, our faith in him, that gives the strength and the courage to do so.

And "I know why the caged bird sings. . . ." Hers is a song of a free spirit trapped against its will, of a being meant for the vastness of the sky but pinned down and trapped in a space so small that sometimes breath itself seems impossible. And what breath there is, is spent screaming (singing?) out frustration, rage, fear, and, hopefully, in the midst of it all, the determination to "make it over."

I see myself growing slower, stiffer, pain-bound, and illness-ridden, and I see so many others—young of body and strong of heart—who are also prevented by lack of opportunity, by the sins of racism and sexism and all other "-isms," from living as they choose, from being the person they would like to be and are capable of being.

And I recognize my calling. It is a calling, a vocation, a request from God. It is a calling to serve others, to learn from my pain and my frustration, to be able to share it with others who also feel trapped (but whose bars are less visible than my own because they have been artificially created and imposed) so that they will realize that they are not alone. I think of women imprisoned for their gender, men and women trapped by others' view of their race, the elderly tossed aside in barren and abusive homes, and so many others captive through no fault of their own.

As my body weakens, my mind grows ever sharper, honed to slice away at the useless and the nonsensical and to do the only thing I can do, "speak the truth," as poet Mari Evans proclaims. I must speak the truth that human beings are not meant to be caged, but to be free, whether black, brown, red, yellow, or white, every color of the rainbow. Whether physically or mentally handicapped, whether male or female, we are all God's creation and are meant to be free. But that freedom must come not only from without, that will come in time. It must first come from within, from the very core of our beings, from the very depths of our soul.

It is not enough to beat against the bars that encircle me, bars made up of my very flesh and bone, because I cannot change them, I cannot free myself in that sense. But I can free myself through my spirit that cannot be vanquished. I can free myself with the power of my words, flying high above and away from my no longer functioning body. Strengthened in spirit, I can serve to free others from the artificial cages in which they have been placed because of their race, their sex, their poverty, their age, or the language they speak or are unable to speak. My words can serve as hammers to beat open the doors so that they can begin their own journey, their own flight of freedom.

It is with my song, with my words, that I break down the barriers that separate me from you. It is the ultimate irony: I, who am a prisoner of my own body, can be a key to open the locked doors of the minds and hearts of others.

Yes, "I know what the caged bird feels, alas!" And I know why it beats its captive wings until they bleed bright drops of blood because I still rage against this crippling disease that has so quickly and quietly made me its captive. But I also "know why the caged bird sings." And I shall continue to sing my song of freedom; I shall fling my prayer of hope for all who are captive against their will, against the very gates of heaven, until I am called home "to be with God." By serving others, I am serving myself and my God; by seeking the liberation of all who are oppressed, I know I shall one day too be free.

# I Believe, Lord, Help My Unbelief

And he said, ". . . have pity on us and help us."
Jesus said to him, "If you are able!—All things can
be done for the one who believes." Immediately
the father of the child cried out, "I believe; help
my unbelief!" (Mark 9:21-24—NRSV).

There are days, but more often nights, when the only
words I can pray, through gritted teeth and streaming
silent tears, are, "Lord, I believe, please, please help my
unbelief." I do believe, Lord, that you have brought me
this far; it is you who have guided my feet at every step
and turning; you who have helped me, no, guided me,
in the decisions I have made that have made my life such
as it is. But there is that other side, that side of fear and
pain and frustration when the hours creep by and still
the dawn has not arrived, or the eyes closed, when the
pain will not cease and I ask why. Why do I believe? Who
is this God that supposedly cares for me? Where is he
when I need him most in my pain and anger and frustration at the constant battling I must do to achieve such
small measures of success?

But I know the answer. Deep down, within my very
being, I know that this God whom I know so well, with
whom I have fought many long and exhausting battles
because I did not tolerate his guidance easily or patiently,
this God is still with me. He has not walked away from

me, I have turned away from him. Turned away because I am tired of the fight, not permanently—at least I pray it is not permanent—but just right now I simply cannot take the burden of being one of God's chosen—chosen not because of some greatness of my own but because God sees in me more than I will ever be able to see in myself. My God calls me forth from within myself and I pretend to be deaf or too busy or too tired, and that certainly is the truth, but my God is patient. He knows me as I know myself, even more so, for he knew me before I was because he was, eternally.

I cry out in my anger, my fear, my pain, my frustration and God listens. He does not always respond, at least not in ways that I can hear or see but, in time, the pain lifts, the sleep comes, the anger dies, the frustration ceases. And I realize that once again, God is holding me like a loving mother in the palm of her hand, easing my troubles, wiping away the doubt and fear and giving me the strength to go on.

My God is a "way maker"; when all ahead is dark and all doors seem closed, faintly a light begins to shine in the far-off distance and, slowly and hesitantly, often against my will, I turn toward it. I turn because I know my God will be there, welcoming, loving, caring, making room for me even though we both know that the time will come yet again when, in pain, in anger, in fear, in frustration, I will turn away from the one who is the source of my life while crying, "O God, I do believe, please, please, please help my unbelief." Yet I know that no matter how often I turn away and cry out, God will be there to soothe it all away and to renew my spirit again.

> Dear Lord,
> When I cry out in fear
> I know you hear not only the fear
>   but the faith which underlies it.

When I cry out in pain
   you hear the passion which undergirds it.
When I cry out in anger,
   you hear the hope that lives deep within me that
   things can and will be different.
Lord, show me the way to hear you
   even when I am deep in despair;
Help me to accept that I can only heal myself
   if I allow you to minister to me in my pain.
Show me thy way, oh Lord;
Help me in my unbelief,
Upheld as it is by my
   deep and profound belief in You.

# *Thy Will, Not Mine, Oh Lord*

"Father, if you are willing, remove this cup from me; yet, not my will but yours be done" (Luke 22:42—NRSV).

It is 7:00 a.m.—the dawn of a new day after another night spent only partially in sleep. I lie awake, tired and achy, wondering why this is happening when so much seemed to be going right. The sky is lightening, the birds are singing merrily, and I am soul-sick and weary.

It is Lent and I can truly empathize with the sufferings of Jesus in my own life. Except that it does not end after forty days and forty nights, it goes on for 365 seemingly endless days and nights.

I wonder about Jesus' journey in those last days of his life. What did he feel, what was he thinking? He was both man and God—the Gospels reveal his fear, his self-doubt, but also his conviction, his acceptance of what was to come even as he prayed for the cup to be taken away from him if at all possible.

I, too, pray that this cup, the burden of chronic illness, of constant pain and limitation, can be taken away, yet with an admittedly heavy heart, I, too, cry at my darkest hour—this time between dark and dawn, "Thy will be done, Oh Lord." Not that it is your will that I suffer this way but that somehow in the suffering I can learn something of value and pass it on, hopefully, to others.

I look at myself these days, the once robust, muscular body of an athletic woman gone, beginning to soften and twist, and I ask myself, "How can I, a cripple, witness to Christ? Can I be a disciple of one who required everything from his followers?" I certainly could not have followed him then. Once a backpacker who would daily walk ten to twelve miles with a forty pound pack and think nothing of it, I cannot today walk four blocks carrying a two pound package without being overwhelmed by exhaustion at day's end. I would not have survived in the deserts of Galilee even half a day.

What is it that God is asking of me as I become one increasingly entrapped by a body that refuses to obey my will, a body that goes its own way? Perhaps my body is a metaphor for my spiritual life as I flee from the sound, the presence of God's call, a call I once responded to with heart-felt joy. Why do I flee? What am I in flight from, God or myself, this stranger in a foreign body that I have become?

How can I witness to Christ, how can I witness to one who was deemed perfect when I am oh so imperfect in body, mind, and yes, even soul? I no longer know myself. I see a stranger with a face weary and drawn and eyes shadowed in pain and I turn away.

I am weak. I am fearful. I love those I should not. I crave things I need not. I am angry, even bitter at times. I wish vengeance and havoc on those who betray not just me, but the helpless ones around me who multiply day by day. Yet I can do nothing.

I myself am at fault. I speak of the poor and homeless, the voiceless and formerly invisible but now all too visible ones, yet I cannot live amongst them for I know I would not survive. I know I could not tolerate the cold, the dirt, the discomfort, the hunger. I am free to choose; they suffer as I do but in far worse conditions not of their own choosing. I have a good job, a good salary, health insurance. How do those in the ghettos, barrios, and reservations of our country survive their illnesses, let alone go on to achieve success in the world?

Am I a hypocrite? Is talking and writing about liberation, both physical and spiritual, enough? Is listening to their cries and trying to convey them to others who can make a difference sufficient, or am I just fooling myself, playing a game, being as hypocritical to those, young and old, who come to me for guidance, for spiritual help, as those others that I denounce for their insensitivity? My tears are not enough. Yet they flow into my words and bring tears to others. But are they then able to act and will they do so?

How can I give when I feel so empty inside? Where is the God I once knew and loved—the "absent" one, as Carretto[1] called God, the one who is eternally present to me but not always when I want him to be. "God may not be there when you want him, but He's right on time" is the understanding of many. Is that the answer to my fears and frustration, to truly "let go and let God"; to realize and accept that my time and God's time may be totally different and that the work I am attempting to do in "my" time may eventually bear fruit in "his"?

I think of the words of the Negro National Anthem that so few know today. It is important to listen and not just mouth the words:

> God of our weary years,
> God of our silent tears,
> Thou who has brought us thus far on our way;
> Thou who has by thy might,
> Led us into thy light,
> Keep us forever in thy path we pray.

---

[1] Carlos Carretto of the Little Brothers of Jesus, a religious order founded by Charles Foucault, himself was accidentally crippled by one of his religious brothers and wrote many spiritual books on the subject of suffering.

This is the faith that sustains me, the faith that has sustained so many. My faith is in a God who answers prayer not necessarily in the way or at the time I may want him to, but who does, in his own time, answer in ways that continue to astound me. This God is one who knows and understands my pain and my fears and who walks beside me always, helping me, guiding me, nurturing me, strengthening me, reassuring me that the work I am attempting is truly God's work as well.

> Oh, God, rest beside me during these days
> and nights of pain.
> Help me to make it through them
> Knowing that on the other side of pain
> is the calming peace of restful sleep.
> Enable me to use this time not to grieve
> the loss of what I once had,
> But to make use of the many other
> gifts with which you have blessed me.
> Show me the way thru this maze
> of pain and grief, Lord;
> Enable my soul to "make it over" the rough places
> and the plain, to find its home in you.

# Let Go and Let God

The mothers of the Black Church, those elderly women who have worked hard all of their lives, often with so little reward, have a way of saying, whenever something goes wrong or someone is burdened more than they felt they could bear, "You just have to 'let go and let God.' " As a child, I would look at these strong Black women who I knew had been through so much in their lives, and who were still going through difficult times, and wonder what they meant. What did it mean to "let go and let God"; let go of what, or was it who? Was it a person, place, or a thing that was supposed to be "let go" of? And what did God have to do with it? Let God what? Do something, say something, be something? It seemed an unanswerable question, a statement lost in the mystery of greater age and wisdom than mine. I must admit I often felt impatient or annoyed when I was advised to "let go and let God, child" because I could not figure out how—or perhaps did not have the patience or faith—to turn my troubles over to a God I was not completely sure of.

Over the years of my growing up, both in and out of the Black Church, but always within the Black community that was its foundation, I slowly began to understand what those old women, who in my mind had seen and experienced it all, meant. They had experienced both the joys and the sorrows that human life has to bring. Yet, they could, when necessary, simply "let go and let God."

They could "let go" of the pain of losing a child through illness or misfortune or of watching another child or their husband slowly give up hope of getting a meaningful job, of having something tangible to produce at day's end. They could "let go" of the racism that confronted them at every turn, of being called out of their rightful name and having to respond humbly to those who were less God-fearing than themselves, and they could "let God" carry those sorrows for a while. God did not take over the pain, the frustration, or the anger—it was still there—but they could rest their burden with the Lord for just a little while until they found the strength to take it up and carry it again. Some would say they were passive; that the older generation did not "let God," but "let" racists step on them while they found refuge in a spiritual realm. But they would be wrong. Some fail to see the strength and courage that "letting go" provided these women; strength and courage that enabled them to, yes, sometimes turn the other cheek, but also to keep fighting for better times for their children and their childrens' children. They were not fighting for themselves but for those coming down the line.

Today, as I battle with my own fears and doubts, my own frustrations (about who I am and where I am going) and yearnings for a life free from pain, free from prejudice and discrimination, free from the constant struggle to survive and simply be me, I have come to realize that there are times when life becomes infinitely more tolerable if the burden is shared, with human friends, yes, but even more importantly, shared with a God who loves and watches over me like a "mother hen brooding over her chicks." It is that same God who has said, "Behold, while you were in your mother's womb, I knew you and I named you. How could I love you less now?"

To "let go and let God" is to put yourself into the hands of God, even for just a little while, until the challenges of life are more bearable. It enables us to step away from the seeming chaos of today's world and to be at peace for a time while we catch our breath. By "letting go" of our earthly cares from time to time, it is so much easier to "let God" help us manage them when once again we are confronted with them and must take them upon our shoulders. It is not a form of "other-worldly" escape, for the pain, the anger, the fears, the frustrations are always, sadly, a part of life, not because God wants it so, but because of our own human failure to make it different.

My God is a "wonder-working God" who shares the burdens of this world with me and, in so doing, helps me to learn of both my strengths and my weaknesses. This strong and loving God reveals to me the way I need to be for those around me—a nurturer, a healer, a sustainer, and a friend.

> Powerful and loving God
> Walk with me this day
>   for just a little while,
> For my body grows weary
>   and my feet falter and stumble.
> I feel overwhelmed by the pressures
>   of my life, the demands of family, career, health,
>   society; all the many things that seem so
>   important and yet are not always as important
>   as I think.
> I lift up my hands and heart to you in faith
>   knowing that when I can no longer carry on
> You will be there to carry me onward.
> Help me to accept my limitations
>   and to acknowledge my weaknesses.
> Help me to recognize my strengths and to use
>   them in ways that are healing and holy for others.
> Help me to "let go" of my problems and concerns
>   and to "let" you be "God."

# *I Surrender All*

All to Jesus I surrender,
All to Him I freely give;
I will ever love and trust Him,
In His presence daily live.

I surrender all,
I surrender all,
All to Thee, my blessed Savior,
I surrender all. (Refrain)

All to Jesus I surrender,
Humbly at His feet I bow;
Worldly pleasures all forsaken,
Take me, Jesus, take me now.

All to Jesus I surrender,
Make me, Savior, wholly Thine;
Let me feel the Holy Spirit
Truly know that Thou art mine.

All to Jesus I surrender,
Lord, I give myself to Thee;
Fill me with Thy love and power,
Let Thy blessings fall on me.[1]

One of the most heart-rending yet comforting songs
I know is one I first heard sung for a friend's celebration

[1] Text: Judson W. Van de Venter, 1855–1939.

of the taking of perpetual vows. It called her and all of us present to surrender all that we were, all that we could be, to the loving arms of Christ Jesus. The song haunts me still as I have sung or heard it sung since and have tried to live out the simple faith proclaimed in its words.

It is a simple song, yet one very profound in its meaning. For me, it calls forth the memory of Jesus' admonition to the poor, young, rich man to sell all his worldly goods and follow him. It is a charge so simple, yet so difficult in its execution that, at times, it plagues me as I go about my day with its melody sounding in my inner being. I, like many others, can sing the song with heartfelt emotion, with tears in my eyes, yet then get up and go about my life, giving little thought to what the words really mean.

> All to Jesus, I surrender,
> All to Him, I freely give;
> I will ever love and trust Him,
> In His presence daily live.

For many, these words are saccharine-sweet and simplistic. They appear to be a plea to be relieved of the burdens of this world and to be gathered into the arms of Jesus in the next, away from the strife, clamor, and pain of this worldly life. But to me, that interpretation is itself simplistic; it is a dualistic, dichotomous way of reading and living out the faith revealed in these innocuous sounding words. Such a reading fails to recognize the deeper meaning of the words that can be seen in terms of the challenge that they truly are; the challenge to surrender oneself, body and soul, but to do so while remaining in the world, enmeshed in all of its pain and chaos. It is a call to follow Christ, to walk in Christ's footsteps, but to do so as Christ himself did, as a vulnerable human being living out his faith in his Father in the world.

I surrender all,
I surrender all,
All to Thee, my blessed Savior,
I surrender all.

What am I being asked to surrender, Lord? You have blessed me with intelligence, with a mind that absorbs, digests, and consumes material and then spits it back out in ways so astounding to me at times that I liken my mind to a computer, a machine that simply takes in and regurgitates on demand. Perhaps that is how I distance myself from you and from the world around me. A computer does not have a conscience; a computer does not need a conscience. It simply inputs and outputs material without having to wonder or worry about the impact of those ideas on others; how they will be affected in their daily lives, whether it will make them better or worse, happy or sad, healthier or sicker.

I walk past the homeless daily with their paper cups and their sad hand-written signs. I automatically feel in my pocket but, usually, I give nothing. I fear the little I have will be of no use to them, but is that truly what I feel or am I simply tired of seeing them, repelled by their noise, their smell, their desperation? What can I give them that will make any difference in their lives? How can I affect the causes that have stranded them here, living their lives in public view?

I surrender all? What must I surrender? My own fears, doubts, and insecurities, my own disdain for those who refuse to see the humanity in me, in people of color, in the poor, in those less fortunate than myself? But what do I really surrender? I live well, I teach at an upper-level, predominantly white school. I am neither poor nor hungry. I read, I write, I teach, I am able to afford not all, but many of the "extras" that life can offer—books, travel, entertainment, nice clothing. What is it that I can offer to you, my God, that is of any particular value set

against the vast needs and cries of the poor, the homeless, the hopeless, those fast disappearing between the
cracks in our thoughtless, self-preoccupied society?

> All to Jesus I surrender,
> Humbly at His feet I bow;
> Worldly pleasures all forsaken,
> Take me, Jesus, take me now.

I can only surrender myself, my faith in you and in
God's creation, my belief and my unbelief in a better
world to come not just after death, but right here on
earth, and my conviction that I do have much to
surrender—my indifference, my longing for solitude, my
need for space, my fear, my anger, my frustration at the
cruel physical limitations that imprison me. I must recognize and surrender my pride in my once perfect, healthy
body; in my ability to do anything that I wanted whenever I wanted to. I must acknowledge my grief and anger
over the loss of personal freedom and the growing de-
pendence on others that is my future. I must surrender
my anger at you and at your Body, the Church, for what
seems at times to be callous indifference to human suffering, realizing that it is truly *man*-made, with all of the
faults and failures but also the promise that can lie in the
human person.

All to you, Jesus, I surrender. I surrender my desire
to be more than I am capable of being; my desire to do
more than I am able to do; my desire to have more than
is necessary for life. For I realize that surrendering is not
giving up. It is not a denial of my self or of my abilities,
but is rather a freeing of self so that I can do more and
be more than I ever thought I was capable of doing or
being. It is the ability to recognize what is truly meaningful and necessary for my life and to do without all that
is not so.

All to Jesus I surrender,
Make me, Savior, wholly Thine;
Let me feel the Holy Spirit
Truly know that Thou art mine.

In return, however, finite and fragile human being that
I am, I do ask for one small thing, the peace of mind that
only you can give, realizing in the asking that to acquire
it requires a constant and conscientious surrender of all
that gets in the way of true peace.

I surrender all,
I surrender all,
All to Thee, my blessed Savior,
I surrender all.

I am yours, Oh Lord, do with me as you will, even
though I admit that I fear what you may ask of me. You,
like the words of this song, call me out of myself; you
stir emotions I thought buried; you awaken within me
a courage I did not know I had, to dare to witness to your
love for all of life, in its joys and in its despair, with my
own.

Oh my God, I cry out to you
    in my confusion and despair.
I want so badly to be your beloved,
    but your love frightens me;
Your love is an all-consuming love
    which allows nothing to be held back.
I fear I cannot surrender to you all and
    everything that I am and hope
    to be because there is so much that
    I do not want to let go.
"Lead me, guide me along thy way,"
For your way, at times, seems so dark and lonely
    and I am afraid.

# *Tired*

## A Prayer of Despair and Hope

I am tired of work, I am tired of building up
   somebody elses' civilization.
Let us take a rest, M' Lissy Jane.
I will go down to the Last Chance Saloon,
   drink a gallon or two of gin,
   shoot a game or two of dice
   and sleep the rest of the night on one
     of Mike's barrels.
You will let the old shanty go to rot,
   the white people's clothes turn to dust,
   and the Calvary Baptist Church sink
     to the bottomless pit.
You will spend your days forgetting you
   married me and your nights hunting the
   warm gin Mike serves the ladies in the
     rear of the Last Chance Saloon.
Throw the children into the river;
   civilization has given us too many.
It is better to die than to grow up
   And find that you are colored.
Pluck the stars out of the heavens.
   The stars mark our destiny.
   The stars marked my destiny.
I am tired of civilization.

—Fenton Johnson[1]

[1] *Poetry of Black America*, 24.

Despair. Hopelessness. Those days when you feel you cannot look at yourself or anyone else one more time. Feeling the tears slide slowly down my face like drips from a leaky faucet, why am I crying? Yet to stop takes so much effort. And I no longer have the energy to make the effort.

Despair—the bleakness of a life where all the doors seem closed, all the tunnels lightless. Hope is no more. There is no use in looking for another way out, for there is only one way out.

And that way is the way you do not want to go— because you have gone that way before and been blinded, blinded by the light of God's face shining before you, leading the way, the way out.

Why am I afraid to follow? All of my life has been spent, unknowingly and unwillingly, in pursuit of God, or so I thought. But in reality, I see that it was God who was pursuing me.

Truly, I am tired of civilization. I am tired of the false lights and phony glitter that lure me from the path, yet it is so difficult to turn away from them to the lonely path you are urging me to walk. I am tired of being the first, the first to achieve "this," the first to accomplish "that"; it is wearing me out, grinding me down, leaving me in a lonely place apart from everyone.

How does one go on, on into the light rather than turn away from it? Where do I find the courage to say yes, yes, and yes again to your constant, patient, loving calling of my name?

I am tired. I weary of trying to make people understand what it means to be me—Black, female—in this white, male world. I am weary of watching the children, my children, though not born of my womb, Black and Brown, children of all races, start out bright and full of hope in their early years only to end up dulled and hopeless by the time they are adolescents. Can it be better that they die young or unborn, never having to face the pain of limitation, of denial, of thwarted dreams? Where am I going, Lord? Where are my people going? Where are we all going, Lord? Why have you called me out into this "howling wilderness" of death and greed and anger and pain? What do you want of me, a cripple, weak of limb yet with a mind filled to bursting with the knowledge of, the pain of, the suffering and growing despair of the people, a people of many races? Where is the kingdom that was promised us? How can I show others the way when I feel lost myself, when I cannot seem to find the door and am unable to see the light?

I cannot bear it alone, Lord, I cannot bear it alone. For what have we suffered all these many years? For what am I suffering now? Why do my hands refuse to cooperate, yet you persist in sending words and more words to my brain that I must put down on paper, hoping someone will read them, hoping someone will be helped by your words in my hand, in my voice? Is there any reason to hope or is there only reason to despair? My hope lies in the dream of a new understanding of "civilization," a new understanding of humanity that does not require the dehumanizing of some and the exalting of only a few. I seek a new vision that uplifts us all, regardless of race, ethnicity, color, or sex. My hope lies in you, Lord, in your vision of a better world to come and in your creation.

Once you walked this earth and created a people— both male and female you created them, of every race and color and hue you created them. And you took joy in that creation. And you loved them. Yet, there are times when it seems we, that same creation, delight in tearing down all that you have built up; in hating what you so dearly loved. Help us to reclaim that joy you felt when you gave us life, loving Mother God. Help us to renew our love of you and each other, loving Father God. Grant that we may regain our hope and our faith, that we may renew our strength, that we might "run and not grow weary," so that once again as a people, a many-nationed and multi-hued people, we may "mount up on eagle's wings" and fly away from that tower of Babel that we created through our own selfishness and greed, a monument to our blindness. Help us to fly toward that "new world a-bornin'" where we all will be granted the dignity and freedom of our shared birthright, our creation in you.

We need your help to create that world, Lord, for so many of us grow tired, so many of us lose faith, and so many of us despair. We destroy instead of building up. We tear down even our own creations like animals chewing off a limb in order to release themselves from a trap. Help us to see that the traps are of our own creation, not yours, and that we are trapping each other in cages of pain, anger, and deceit. Show us the way.

Show me the way. Help me to look once again into the blinding light of your love so that I may, somehow, someway, walk with my people, all of God's people, into the light. With your guidance, with your strength surrounding me, "shoring me up on every leaning side," I know I will be able to continue to work with others toward the day when that new world will be born. It will be born within our very midst and we will all rejoice in its birth together as one people of many colors but of one faith, however we may name you, in one loving and liberating God.

# I Don't Feel No Ways Tired

I don't feel no ways tired,
I come too far from where I started from,
Nobody told me that the road would be easy,
I don't believe He brought me this far to leave me.
(Refrain)

I've been friendless, but God brought me.
I've been lonely, but God brought me.

Please, don't leave me, don't leave me, Jesus.
Don't leave me, don't leave me, Lord.

I don't believe that God would bring me,
I don't believe that God would bring me,
I don't believe that God would bring me this far
just to leave me.[1]

Liberation comes in all shapes and forms. There is the physical release from pain that comes in death—quick and sudden or slow and tedious, but release eventually comes and one can "go home and be with God."

Then there is the liberation that comes from a deeply-held faith in a God who saves, a "wonder-working" God, a God who can make everything all right, who frees us from the many pains and problems of the day and enables us to go on about our business of helping to bring about the coming of the Kin-dom.

[1] Text: Curtis Burrell.

There is the liberation of sharing one's life with another, of being able to "let go" at times, knowing the one with whom you have pledged to live and share your future will step in and hold on for a while and that, in turn, you can and will do the same for him or her.

There is liberation in death; there is liberation in faith; there is liberation in love. There is also liberation in struggling to make a positive difference in the lives of others, even when your own seems to be "going to hell in a handbasket." I do not mean a life of martyrdom or extreme sacrifice, simply a life of being lovingly present to others when they are seeking answers, when they are trying to "make it over" into the Kin-dom, when they are seeking the right way to go and need guidance in choosing their next steps, need a listening ear and a caring heart even when you, yourself, are so tired and weary that each step seems like an uphill climb.

It is freeing—a painful freedom perhaps—to realize that God can and does speak through you even at times when you feel God is farthest away from you.

My life has been so difficult of late that I have felt isolated and apart from God. The old friendly camaraderie and kinship I used to feel has disappeared and nothing seems to be rushing in to take its place. There is an emptiness within me that once was filled, a hollowness that once was solid, a yearning that once was fulfilled. And I mourn the loss from within that emptiness, within that hollowness, within that yearning.

At times I feel deserted by God, left alone in this harsh world to struggle with my now clumsy and blinded body toward the light that once shined so brightly.

But then I am asked to speak to others of what I have learned in my seemingly slow and painful journey toward Christ, and something miraculous happens. Words come, words that somehow seem to lift people's hearts, words that lighten their burdens and give them the relief of tears, words that give them hope and wonder, and I realize that

God is still here, within me, giving me voice.

The emptiness, the hollowness, the yearning I feel is caused, I realize, by my own inability to accept and acknowledge the new me that is being built out of the fragmented mold of the person I once was. I am no longer whole; I am no longer able. I lean upon the Lord and others because I must, and I hate that because it demeans the image I have of myself as a free and independent being.

Yet I realize, as I see and feel the reactions of those around me when I speak words inspired by God alone, that I am still free, I am still independent. But it is a new freedom, a new independence, a freeing of myself to be used by God as an instrument, as a sounding board—but not a passive one, No! For I struggle and fight and yell and scream against that usage, yet when it happens, oh, the peace, the liberating, restful peace that flows throughout me and revives my soul again. And I wonder at my fears and my angers and, most especially, at my self-doubt, my feelings of unworthiness at being used in this way.

It is exhausting; it is wearing me out—this constant struggle. I want to hear God's voice directly within me as once I used to, a voice that guided and sustained me in my journey. I want God to talk to me, not through me. Yet, when I stop struggling and fighting, I realize that I am simply moving one step further on my own journey and one step closer to that promised liberation, when all of humanity is truly made one. My prayer, then, is to use me, Lord, again and again if it means others will not suffer, others will have their hopes renewed, their faith enriched. And I begin to hear once again those words that have sustained me throughout the years of my journeying toward God:

I don't feel no ways tired.
I come too far from where I started from,

Nobody told me that the road would be easy,
I don't believe He brought
me this far to leave me.

I do feel tired at times, but the tiredness is only phys-ical and it soon lifts for I realize that the road I have chosen is one to which I have been guided from afar. Although at times I feel forsaken and alone, I know God is still guiding me, for life has brought me a "mighty long way." God has faith in me even when, especially when, I have no faith of my own.

# I Couldn't Hear Nobody Pray

And I couldn't hear nobody pray: (O Lord!)
And I couldn't hear nobody pray,
O way down yonder by myself
And I couldn't hear nobody pray. (Refrain)

In the valley! (A couldn't hear nobody pray.)
On my knees! (A couldn't hear nobody pray.)
With my burden! (A couldn't hear nobody pray.)
And my Savior! (A couldn't hear nobody pray.)

O Lord!
Chilly waters! (A couldn't hear nobody pray.)
In the Jordan! (A couldn't hear nobody pray.)
Crossing over! (A couldn't hear nobody pray.)
Into Canaan! (A couldn't hear nobody pray.)

O Lord!
Hallelujah! (A couldn't hear nobody pray.)
Troubles over! (A couldn't hear nobody pray.)
In the kingdom! (A couldn't hear nobody pray.)
With my Jesus! (A couldn't hear nobody pray.)
O Lord![1]

I lost a friend today, God. Actually, it did not just happen today, suddenly, out of the blue. It was more a wearing away of the edges of our friendship, caused by

[1] Text: African American spiritual.

distance, changes in lifestyles, changes in dreams, even changes in belief, until the fabric of our love for each other suddenly tore apart right before our eyes.

I do not even know if she is aware of the loss yet. I do not know how to tell her. She no longer seems open to my dreams. She seems intolerant of my pain and frustration. I can understand that, Lord; we had even talked about it before our last visit. I guess I wanted to alert her to the changes in me, in my health, changes that would end, once and for all, our plans to roam the mountains and the valleys of life around us.

She was too busy to listen, Lord, so full of her own plans and dreams that I always listened to faithfully even though I sometimes had no deep interest in them, even though they did not involve me, even though she talked of people like things to be moved around on a chart that she had made, with no life or will or desire or dreams of their own.

And when I began, tentatively then with increasing vigor, to talk of my hopes and plans for the future, of my dreams even though I realized they would possibly never come to fruition, she refused to listen. She grew angry and accused me of insensitivity. She wanted to comment and critique, but they were dreams! You do not comment on or critique dreams, you listen in silence, you nod your head, and in love you allow the dreamer to dream, even though you know the dream may be forever beyond them.

I felt so betrayed. I felt stepped on and humiliated, manipulated, told to "stay in my place," wherever that place was. I had occasionally felt that from her before when she would assume her way was the only way and, therefore, the best way. It would cause cold silences to fall between us, silences filled with the tension of suppressed anger and pain, the weight of unspoken angry words.

But I have changed, too, as this insidious disease takes its toll on me. I have become, if anything, even more introspective, even more sensitive to the unspoken thoughts and feelings of others. This disease has frightened me, but it has also challenged me. It has challenged me to have continued faith in that which cannot be seen nor heard, felt nor tasted. It has challenged my faith in you.

All, all it seems that I have loved in life has been taken away from me now and I could only stand by and watch them leave: the man I loved so fiercely yet who seemed so afraid of my love, and whose love I also feared, who left me without a word; the woman, my friend for so long, who turned into a cruel, humiliating stranger before my very eyes; my strong and beautiful hands of which I was, perhaps vainly, so proud; my body, my own flesh and blood, with which I once could climb mountains and run and leap and play and can now, on some days, barely will to move.

> O way down yonder by myself
> And I couldn't hear nobody pray.

I went to her in need, as someone to pray with me and for me, and found she no longer believed—whether in you or your Church, the Body of your Son, Jesus, I am not sure. But it brought such an agonizing emptiness to me because she could neither understand nor accept my continued love for you and your Church despite all that has happened to me.

Is there no one left with whom I can pray? Is there no one who will pray for me? I know there are but they are so far away and so busy with their own lives, it seems too much to ask them to bear the burden of my own fears and pain as well. Or is it that I fear to ask, knowing that it will mean baring my soul anew and risking rejection and denial?

I am way down here, Lord, all by myself, and I cannot seem to hear anyone praying, not even myself. Yet there are still times, when a bird sings on a sunny spring day or a child looks at me with innocent love or someone says how much some few words I have said have meant to them, that I realize that I am praying, quietly, silently, passionately, and painfully, but I am praying, deep within my soul, and that you do hear my prayer.

Out of the grief over a lost friendship comes the comfort of a friendship that is always with me, that will never leave me, no matter what I do or fail to do. And I understand once again how my ancestors, poor, illiterate Black men and women who did not even own themselves, could sing so long ago, while deep in a valley of fear and despair, words of despair and hope at the same time.

Hallelujah!
Troubles over!
In the kingdom!
With my Jesus!

I know that new troubles will arise, new sorrows will emerge, friendships will be lost and maybe somehow, hopefully, even restored, but if I continue to walk "with my Jesus," I, too, shall "make it over" to the Promised Land—a land not just way off in glory somewhere but a land of promise right here and right now, freeing me to continue to be about my Creator's work.

Loving Father and Mother God,
When I find myself in deep despair,
Hurting over an unexpected loss,
Wondering if I will ever have
    a friend to confide in,
To share my dreams again;
You remind me that you are always there,
Silently waiting, quietly listening;

And the pain is lessened, the fears subside,
And I rest easy in your loving arms.

Thank you, my Jesus, for always being my friend.
Give me the courage to continue holding out
A hand of friendship, of love
To those men and women, so like myself,
Who persist in dreaming
   even though they realize they may only
   be dreaming dreams.

# That Good Night

I will "*not* go gently into that good night," but will continue to "rage against the dying of the light." In the words of the Welsh poet Dylan Thomas I find surprising strength. I have always found strength in them long before I ever thought or knew I would have need of them.

Thomas' words apply to his father who is dying, gently, quietly, seemingly willingly, whether of old age or disease I do not know. He begs, pleads, screams at him to fight against this death that is not gentle, but comes as a thief in the night, stealing him away from those who love and, perhaps more importantly, need him.

My "death," because that is how I see it, is not a final one. In many ways, that would be so much simpler and perhaps even easier to bear. My death is that of the person I once knew—myself—who was full of life and energy and vitality. I was a woman who loved to run and hike, to swim and canoe, to ski and climb mountains, and who can do none of these now without great loss of energy, without verging on collapse, without an exhaustion that is almost unbearable because it is so pervasive, without constant and often unbearable pain.

I rage against the "dying," the dying of the vigorous, athletic, able woman that I knew, that I loved (perhaps wrongly because indeed it was a form of vanity), that woman of whom I was so proud. I was proud of her because she could do anything, take on any task, work till she "dropped," but she never did. I believed myself to be, and saw myself as, one of the strong Black women, like so many others of my race who laid the foundations for the survival of my people in this country, but at what cost to themselves in body and soul?

I conveniently forget the days of severe menstrual pain against which I could not fight, the days when some of the hills seemed more like mountains, the aches and pains, the bruises and concussions, the strains and sprains that occurred all too often. I forget them because they were fleeting; they did not last, and once they ended I could rise again and go out into my beloved woods and float down my beloved streams and find God in all of it.

So where do I turn now in search of God? My God, the one with whom I chatted and sang, with whom I walked in the gardens and woods, *was* a God of the mountains and their streams. He was only to be found, I thought, in the high and desolate places, where the sounds of the city, the screams of those in pain, the rage of those in torment, could no longer be heard.

But I was wrong. When I could no longer run away to the hills and valleys, to the streams and rivers, I found that my God was still with me, indeed, had never left me. For my God is a good God who watches over me wherever I am and who calls me out of myself, out of my fears and self-doubts. When I fear God is absent from me, it is because I have absented myself from God. Yet there is really nowhere I can go and be apart from God. I recognize the truth in the words of one of my favorite songs:

> Ain't no mountain high enough,
> Ain't no river wide enough,
> Ain't no valley low enough
> To keep me from you.

Only I can keep you from me, God. Only I, in my rage and anger and despair, can close the doors and windows of my heart and shut you out. I know, however, that you are right outside (if not actually still within me), patiently waiting, allowing me to rage, allowing me—perhaps even encouraging me—to scream, to cry, to free the grief that lingers within me, to mourn at the "dying of the light."

My God, you know me as I do not know myself; before I was born, you knew me. You know I cannot go quietly. I do not understand the reason for the pain, for the weakening of my body. I listen to the doctors as they speak of heredity and genetics, of stresses and strains, but I am unable to accept their words. At times I cannot stand the frustration of a mind, active and alive, in a body growing slower and less able to keep up with my thoughts, my plans, my dreams. I want to be free, to write all the words that are tumbling around in my head, to set down the thoughts and ideas that come to me when I least expect them. Yet my hands will no longer obey my commands, my fingers swell and hurt, my wrists grow stiff and my shoulders ache. I cannot write, I cannot type, and I hear the thoughts crashing around until they fall, spent and useless, trapped within me.

But I know you, God. I know you and I love you, as you know me, despite my anger, my rage, my frustration, and my fears. I have to admit I cannot, right now, deal with or even accept the understanding that "God does not give you more than you can bear." Perhaps I never will because I do not believe that you are the cause of my illness. Rather, you are the source of my ability to deal with it. But right now, Lord, it all really does feel like too much of a load for me to carry alone. I need your help to carry me through.

I am tired of the struggle, Lord, yet I know that I will continue to struggle because I know the voice within me that urges me to "rage against the dying of the light" is your voice—reminding me that you are and will be with me, even to the very end, whenever and however it may come.

Lord, I ask you once again for the strength
   "to keep on keepin' on."
You have brought me a "mighty long way."
Yet I know there is still a long way to go.
I do not know where you are leading me,
   nor do I understand
   why I must suffer so on the journey.
Yet I recognize in your son Jesus the same fears
   and frustrations, the same pain, anger,
   and loneliness as he journeyed "home" to you.
And I cry out to you yet again and again: "I believe,
   dear Lord, help my unbelief."

# Come, Ye Disconsolate

## A Prayer for My People

Come, ye disconsolate, where'er ye languish—
Come to the mercy seat, fervently kneel;
Here bring your wounded hearts, here tell your anguish:
Earth has no sorrow that heav'n cannot heal.

Joy of the desolate, light of the straying,
Hope of the penitent, fadeless and pure!
Here speaks the Comforter, tenderly saying,
"Earth has no sorrow that heav'n cannot cure."

Here see the Bread of Life, see waters flowing
Forth from the throne of God, pure from above;
Come to the feast of love—come ever knowing
Earth has no sorrow but heav'n can remove.[1]

The birds are singing, the sky is blushing far off on the horizon, a new day is coming, and once again I am awake to see and hear it all. I am weary, so weary, yet sleep once again escapes me. It has been this way for seven days now. I am unable to fall asleep and I lie in my bed, tossing and turning, listening to the radio or tapes or just the sound of silence, eventually giving up and taking down a book or picking up pen and paper and working through the night. Then I stumble through the day, half awake, praying that this night, surely, I will

[1] Text: Stanzas 1–2, Thomas Moore, 1779–1852; stanza 3, Thomas Hastings, 1784–1872.

sleep, yet dreading its coming until I lie awake once again, too weary even for tears.

My mind never seems to weary though. As I lie awake, it begins to go over the day behind or ahead, making plans, thinking of new ideas for books or articles or simply pondering the ways of the world. And I despair because I know that once my brain starts clicking, sleep will never come. Yet even in my despair I become energized because the ideas that come, the thoughts that engage me, are fruitful ones that, once I have regained my balance of sleep, I will be able to put into meaningful action.

This night I went to bed with images that, even in their horror, have become sadly commonplace in today's world: a child beaten to death by an adult, a young man facing life in prison for a gratuitous act of violence, a world at war in various regions, children dying for lack of food in a world of plenty. And I wonder why.

Why all of this needless suffering, Lord? What is the good of it? There can be none; there can be no greater purpose in the senseless taking of life that goes on, seemingly nonstop, throughout this world that you created with such love.

Why have we fallen so far? Why do we seemingly delight in destruction? Who has the answers, Lord? Where will the hope come from?

I look at the children, Lord, and I listen to them. They no longer believe in you as I do. They want proof, tangible evidence, of your promise of a better world. They appear incapable of faith, of taking that leap over the abyss of doubt into your arms. Yet they so desperately seek what they so vehemently deny. They seek love, they seek affirmation, they seek assurance that they are of value in the eyes of others. How do we adults, who have made such a mess of this world, give them that love, that affirmation, that assurance that they so desperately need? How do we heal their wounded hearts?

Come, ye disconsolate, where'er ye languish,
Come to the mercy seat, fervently kneel.
Here bring your wounded hearts, here tell your anguish:
Earth has no sorrow that heav'n cannot heal.

When I feel despondent, as I seem to do so often lately, I think of the words of this song and I think of the children. I have lived a life, short as it has been, full of love and promise despite the physical limitations that have plagued me throughout. I remember the days when I wandered through the woods and valleys after giving up on the institutional Church that I had been brought up in because it seemed so sterile, so—I felt then—hypocritical. I left the Church but I found another, a natural one where the forests of tall, masted trees were my cathedrals and the rocks and boulders strewn across the landscape were the pews. The waters flowing through were holy to me and I heard your voice in the wind, in the singing of the birds, even in the rumbling of the storm clouds, and I was at peace.

Today the earth is full of sorrow, Lord; it is over-burdened with grief and pain, with violence and anger and actions that arise from a sense of despair, of dislocation, of alienation; for the land itself is weeping for the rape of its treasures, the assault on itself. There is no belonging here. The children, especially those in the cities but even those in our sterile, well-planned suburbs, do not know your many and beautiful faces. They, in the cacophony of our cities and the blandness of our suburbs, in their empty lots and crowded malls, have never had the space to simply "be" and allow you to enter their being.

Few have ever seen you revealed in the glory of a sunrise or smiling gently over them in a rainbow of colors after a rain storm. Their lives have been so organized with programs, classes, tutors, or so disorganized by wars in their very back yards, that there is no time to be children, no field but empty, garbage strewn lots, nowhere to experience your wonder unblemished or unadorned.

It was the experience of feeling your presence around me in the quiet of a moonlit night that kept me close to you. How do I, a woman who walks and talks with God, share my journeying with these "lost" children of all ages so that they, too, may come to know you as I have?

They see no future here. They sing not of hope and love, but of fury and pain. They pray not for a renewed life, but simply for an end to lives that have become burdensome and without value. We are losing them to drugs, to the disease of AIDS, to suicide, to abuse—both physical and mental—to so many evils that no one, least of all children, should be exposed to. The children are dying, Lord; words alone no longer reach them, and with each of their deaths, we also die.

Joy of the desolate, light of the straying,
Hope of the penitent, fadeless and pure!
Here speaks the Comforter, tenderly saying,
"Earth has no sorrow that heav'n cannot cure."

They do not hear, Lord. They cannot understand. They do not believe. They cannot be comforted because they cannot recognize the Comforter. They see only the sorrow and have no faith in a heaven that cannot be seen, touched, tasted. They are not interested in abstractions, in learned discussions on the being and essence of God. They simply want to experience you in their lives, acting, being, comforting, consoling. They have no joy; they cannot find the light; they have lost their way.

Whose fault is it? Surely not the children's for they are but children. Is it ours, the adults, their parents and elders who chafed at the "old-fashioned" discipline of our own parents, who resented the "attention" of the older adults, especially those who were not really kinfolk? Why did we stop teaching them the "truth"? Why did we stop loving them into life and begin loving them into death by allowing them freedoms no child should have because they are not capable of using them wisely?

When did we give up on the grandparents, the aunts and uncles, the cousins and godparents who came and went through our own young lives, sometimes causing pain, yes, but more often bringing a gentle, guiding wisdom handed down from generation to generation, from mother to son and father to daughter? When did we give up on our own children, Lord, and why?

As African-Americans, unwelcome residents in this land despite our centuries-long presence here, we have had to struggle to survive. But our struggle has been supported, buoyed up, by our faith, a faith we have persisted in for centuries. Yet today we seem to have lost even that. How can the children believe if we do not believe ourselves? How can the children have hope when we have, somewhere along the line, lost our own?

We are faltering now, Lord, following in the dark, unsure of our way. Our steps are weary as we look ahead and see the same obstacles that we climbed over or worked our way around thirty, fifty, one hundred years ago.

Where is your justice, Lord? Where is your wrath? Why do we continue to suffer while false messiahs—spouting the words of the very ones who have held us in bondage for so long, yet wearing our skin and born of our flesh—crop up on every side? Is it any wonder that the children are falling away when there are no arms to uphold them, no love to sustain them, no hope to bear them up?

We need a Comforter, Lord. We need a judge; one to hold your people, of all races, up to the mirror of their sins and failures. We need a judge to remind us of the promise this nation once was, a promise written, it seems, in dust and soon washed away as we turn our backs on the new immigrants who are so different—in color, in customs, in faiths—than those who came before.

We need your Spirit, Lord, to walk the land calling all of its people forth to repent, to take heed, to prepare yet again the way of the Lord. We need a sign, Lord, for those who have fallen away and given up and for those who have failed in their responsibility to love their God and their neighbor as themselves; who have failed to teach the children to walk in your way because they no longer know the way themselves.

> Here see the Bread of Life, see waters flowing
> Forth from the throne of God, pure from above;
> Come to the feast of love—come ever knowing
> Earth has no sorrow but heav'n can remove.

Show us the way, Oh Lord, for we your people have strayed from your path and wander, blinded and speechless, senseless and unfeeling, in the desert of self-hate and self-destruction; we wallow in the mire of greed and lustful desires. Guide us, Lord, back to the Gospel feast. Open our eyes and unseal our lips so that we may taste once again the Bread of Life and be refreshed and renewed. Re-awaken in us the love for all of your creation in all of its forms that we all once knew so long ago, and teach us to cherish anew the intertwined web of life that sustains us all.

Bless us with new hearts of flesh that will feel the pain of the children, of the aged, of the neglected and cast-off humanity that we have fostered and ill-treated. Welcome them into the family of humanity to which we all belong.

We need you more than ever today, Lord. Although we come to you with different dreams, speaking different languages, worshipping you in different ways, calling you by different names; allow us to see that you are

God, the one God, in whom all of creation rejoices. Help us, Lord, to redeem ourselves in your sight so that we may enter that new world that has been promised to all who believe in you.

The birds are still singing and, though weary in body, I am once again refreshed in spirit by the prayer that has come to me through you. My illness no longer allows me to walk those woods and valleys where once I heard your voice, but I have learned to seek you out wherever I may be and you have always been there. Although I can do little about the physical disease that is robbing me of my body, I thank you for continuing to shed your light within my soul so that I may, with my words, reach out to you and through you to all who suffer—mentally, physically, spiritually, and all other ways.

# One Day at a Time

> One day at a time,
> Sweet Jesus,
> Is all I'm asking of you.
> Just give me the strength
> to do everything
> that I have to do.

"One day at a time . . ." For someone as intelligent as I supposedly am, it has suddenly occurred to me, as I sit sleepily this morning trying to orient myself after a half-sleepless night, that since the onslaught of this disease I have never had an entire week uninterrupted by pain, insomnia, or just a lack of energy to make it through the week. Yet I persist in making plans and developing schedules for myself that someone in perfect physical and mental health would find daunting.

"One day at a time, sweet Jesus . . ." I am slowly and painfully beginning to realize that even "one day" may be too much to ask. Some days, one hour or two is all that I can manage before I have to lie down, completely prostrated by pain or fatigue.

These are the times that truly test my spirit. There is always so much to do. As a professor fast approaching tenure at a major university; as one of only a handful of Black Catholic Theologians in the United States; as someone who others feel is a good listener, mentor, and spiritual guide, my days and evenings are crowded with classes, committee meetings, faculty meetings, meetings with students who come for academic and spiritual assistance.

Yet to whom can I turn, Lord, for guidance, for solace, for company? The days pass so quickly and I see and feel myself struggling under the strain because, belatedly, I realize that I have been pushing myself for so long, for so many years, always assuming that one day there would be time for rest, for a week or two of blessed peace. But that day never seems to come.

> Yesterday's gone, sweet Jesus
> And tomorrow may never be mine.
> Just give me the strength to take everything
> One day at a time.

You are my strength, Lord, and my companion in time of need. You are always there with a listening ear, a welcoming and healing heart. Others, like myself, are so busy, our lives crowded with meetings and plans that we think are so important. And they are, for we are the workers attempting to sow the seeds and gather the bounty of your harvest. Yet, at the same time, we, or at least I, must recognize that the journey can only be traveled "one day at a time." If I push myself too far, there will be one less sower of seeds, one less person to share and spread your word of truth. That will happen in time anyway, but there is no need to rush the inevitable, to chase after death or complete collapse.

I need to recognize and accept my own struggle, Lord, as I counsel others to do and, having done so, continue to get on with my life, a life spent in pilgrimage toward you.

> Help me, Lord, to take this journey
> One day at a time

Recognizing that that day can be divided into
    smaller and smaller parts,
And that each one does not have to be filled to the
    brim with plans and programs and activities.
Continue to help me to see and accept my
    limitations, so that I may continue the good
    work you have begun in me
without losing sight of its goal—a resting place
    with you.
Let me not be pressured into seeking that resting
    place sooner than I need to,
Realizing that there is yet work
    that I must complete here before I move on.
Show me how to walk in your time, my God,
    where a day is just a minute and years
    fly by like hours.
"One day at a time, sweet Jesus
That's all I'm asking of you."
Grant me the strength, the patience and the
    fortitude to continue my journey—
"one day at a time."

# *Fix Me, Jesus, Fix Me*

Oh, fix me (Jesus); Oh, fix me (Jesus);
Oh, fix me; fix me, Jesus, fix me. (refrain)

Fix me for my long white robe. (Fix me, Jesus, fix me.)
Fix me for my starry crown. (Fix me, Jesus, fix me.)

Fix me for my journey home. (Fix me, Jesus, fix me.)
Fix me for my dying bed. (Fix me, Jesus, fix me.)[1]

There are days when I can only murmur the words:

Oh, fix me; Jesus
Oh, fix me; Jesus
Oh, fix me; Jesus
Fix me, Jesus, fix me.

And a vision appears before me of a young, Black male, tall, supple, and lithe—a dancer—as he brings the pain and agony of his world and mine to life.

I first heard this song and saw it performed by the Alvin Ailey Dance Company in Ailey's piece, "Revelations." That was many years ago, but the image has remained—and will always be—with me. Long before I knew pain; long before I gave any thought to my own body's treachery, I watched a young Black man, garbed in white, dance his pain before the world, and I felt it so keenly that I cried.

[1] Text: African American spiritual.

64

Oh, fix me; Jesus
Oh, fix me; Jesus
Oh, fix me; Jesus
Fix me, Jesus, fix me.

My body has aged now, much faster than my mind that is still young and dreams of dancing and running and climbing hills and all of the wonderful, freeing things I once did with a body that, like that young man's, was strong and firm and healthy.

And sometimes it is too much. I grow weary. And I pray:

Fix me for my long white robe,
Fix me, Jesus, fix me.
Fix me for my starry crown,
Fix me, Jesus, fix me.

Yet I know that is a role I am really not ready for and a crown I am totally unprepared for. I have not lived my life yet. There are so many more things I would like to achieve: books I hope to write, classes I want to teach, young people—and old—whose minds I want to help awaken to the sheer joy of learning simply for the pleasure of it.

To open a book and travel back worlds; to see life as others have lived it and to find yourself in those worlds, in those lives, to find yourself shaped and molded by those who have gone before you, the heroes and sheroes who lived their lives and died so that we, too, might live today.

Then the pain begins anew, assaulting me from my blind side, catching me unaware just as I have planned to take a further adventurous step on my journey of knowledge or just after I have finished a round of travel and lectures that have left me filled with hope for the future of my people, my Church, and my world. And the words rise up within me once again:

> Fix me for my journey home,
> Fix me, Jesus, fix me.
> Fix me for my dying bed,
> Fix me, Jesus, fix me.

But the malaise soon passes because I know I am not truly ready for that homeward journey; I have not lived my life to its fullest, a fullness not found, for me, in giving birth to children of my body, but to be found in giving birth, with God's help, to children of my soul. These children, of all ages, of all races and ethnicities, hopefully, hear the good news I am trying to transmit, and accept it as a seed to be buried deep within them, to bloom, as mine did, when they least expect it.

> Oh yes, fix me, Jesus, fix me.
> Fix me so that I can walk on
>     a little while longer.
> Fix me so that I can pray on
>     just a little bit harder.
> Fix me so that I can sing on
>     just a little bit louder.
> Fix me so that I can go on despite the pain,
>     the fear, the doubt, and, yes, the anger.
> I ask not that you take this cross from me,
>     only that you give me the strength to continue
> carrying it onward 'til my dying day.
>     Oh, fix me, Jesus, fix me.

# There Is a Balm in Gilead

There is a balm in Gilead
To make the wounded whole,
There is a balm in Gilead
to heal the sin-sick soul. (Refrain)

Sometimes I feel discouraged
And think my work's in vain,
But then the Holy Spirit
Revives my soul again.

If you cannot preach like Peter,
If you cannot pray like Paul,
You can tell the love of Jesus,
And say, "He died for all!"

Don't ever feel discouraged,
For Jesus is your friend;
And if you lack for knowledge
He'll ne'er refuse to lend.[1]

Five years ago, in the month of my birth, the original diagnosis of my illness, severe chronic rheumatoid arthritis, was confirmed by a doctor upon my return to the United States to attend the Sixth National Black Catholic Congress.

After hearing his confirming diagnosis, I left for southern Maryland to spend some time with my aunt. Her

[1] Text: Jer 8:22; African American spiritual.

home, originally built as a summer retreat, had become for me a place of peace and refuge while I was studying theology in D. C., and I often went there when I felt overwhelmed and confused by the many twists and turns my life was taking in my efforts to respond to what I felt then, and continue to feel now, is a call from God to service. I often jokingly referred to the place as my retreat home.

How ironic those words seemed during those days as I sat and stared out over the brown waters of the Wicomico River, whose beauty had always eased my fears and doubts, and tried to come to some understanding of this sudden assault to my senses.

I was quite literally in a state of shock, a shock overlaid not just with anger and frustration, but with a rage that left me staggering in its wake. Why? Why me? Why now when everything seemed to be going so well for me? The chondromallatia (a disintegrative condition in my knees), which had plagued the first stumbling steps of my journey into the Catholic faith and theological study, was in remission. I had laid down my crutches and braces and been able to walk longer distances and even do a little hiking—nothing dramatic, but enough to give me hope that perhaps I would one day be able to walk once again in my beloved mountains, in the places where I had first truly encountered and heard the still small voice of God calling me forth into this mystery yet still unfolding.

Now this, a disease I thought only struck the elderly whereas I had just turned forty years of age. At first, I refused to accept it, I was simply unable to grasp its overwhelming implications, but the evidence was too great, witnessed to by my increasingly stiff and fumbling fingers, the stiffness in my hips, back, legs, and shoulders, and the pain, the incredible, breath-taking pain that made me a captive in a living, breathing nightmare.

Seven years have now passed. In those seven years, I have managed to complete my dissertation, begin working as an assistant professor of Theology, be promoted to associate professor with tenure, and, to my utter amazement, become a fairly popular public speaker who seems to say words that answer other's questions, that ease their fears and soothe their doubts while my own continue to flutter around and through me seemingly unanswered, uneased, and unsoothed. And I continue to write.

I began these "soul prayers" during a night of sleeplessness caused by the sudden ravaging of pain throughout my body. I end them the same way, at 4:25 a.m. on a Thursday (actually Friday), after two days of lying trapped within a body that refuses to allow me to move freely. Yet in the writing of these brief prayers of my soul, as I look back over the past years and realize that I have managed—despite the pain, despite the fear, despite the self-doubt—to go forward, to forge new ground in my life even while my body, the shell that encases my increasingly liberated soul, goes seemingly backward, becoming weaker and more fragmented and clumsy, I realize that I have never been alone.

> Never Alone
> I don't have to worry 'cause I'm
> Never Alone . . .
> Oh, He walks beside me everyday
> He guides my footsteps in every way.

Throughout this long and sometimes tedious but never boring journey that has been my life, there has always been an Other upon whom I could call, in whose arms I could rest my aching body until the pain went away, one to whom I could entrust all the anxiety and qualms that constantly beset me, one who has been with me all the way.

The words of one song in particular, like a prayer, keep going through my mind tonight:

> How I got over,
> how I got over,

> my soul looks back and wonders,
> how I got over.[2]

This refrain, I realize now, has truly been my constant companion, a continuous murmuring undercurrent through the years of struggling with the pain and frustration of my battle—at times less than successful—with this tenacious disease. I have very often looked back and wondered how in God's name I have gotten over the obstacles and pitfalls—physical, intellectual, social, and all others—that lay in my path. It is a prayer, I realize, that will continue to accompany me until my journey's end even though I realize that I have, intuitively, known the answer all along.

How did I get over all that seemed to be trying to prevent my soul's journey, my efforts to live up to the call that I have received? How else but with the aid and guidance, the eternal, gentle (and sometimes not so gentle!) guidance of a God whose love for me knows no bounds. I have sung these words many times but now I live them for truly I know that

> There is a balm in Gilead
> to make the wounded whole,
> there is a balm in Gilead,
> to heal the sin-sick soul.

Whenever I get laid low by pain, anger, frustration, impatience (and being human I know it will continue to happen), I think of the words of my people—enslaved for so many years without apparent hope—who suffered even more than I ever will at the whims of a fickle master over whom they had little or no control, yet who sang out under a hot and relentless sun:

---

[2] Text: Clara Ward, 1924–1973; copyright 1951 by Andrea Music Co., Philadelphia, Pa.

Sometimes I feel discouraged
and think my work's in vain,
but then the Holy Spirit,
revives my soul again.

Yes, there is a balm in Gilead that soothes my anguish
when, soul-sick and weary, I rail against the shackles my
own flesh have become for me and that sometimes seem
to threaten the very core of my being, the tenuous hold
I maintain between my mind and my heart. Yet I know
that I should never feel totally discouraged, because

. . . Jesus is (my) friend
and if (I) look for knowledge,
He'll never refuse to lend.

I have been in search of knowledge throughout my
life, knowledge that came from books, the words of
others, and from my own lived experience as a Black lay
Catholic woman in a world all too often disposed against
those of my race, of my sex, often of my faith, and even
sometimes of my lay status. But it was not until I began
slowly and haltingly to attempt to write words of my
own, words that spoke of my life and that of my people,
words that gave me a voice, a visibility, a liberation, did
I fully realize that my search had been, and continues to
be, in its deepest sense, a search for knowledge of the
eternal and everlasting love of God, my Savior, the true
and only "lover of my soul."

I know now that the words I write and those I speak
come from that lover, who has called me forth to spread
the good news through the witness of my own weak and
clumsy body.

If you cannot preach like Peter,
if you cannot pray like Paul,
you can tell the love of Jesus,
and say "He died for all."

There is, indeed, a balm in Gilead that eases the anguish of my soul and enables me to continue "getting over" even as my soul, in awe, continues to "look back and wonder." That balm continues to ease the pain of my journey, soothe the murmurings of my fearful heart and lay a cooling solace over the heat of the battles in which I find myself thrust, oftentimes unwillingly, to live a life of witness to Christ Jesus.

I thank you, Jesus,
for the gift of words,
for the power of speech,
for enabling and empowering me to touch the
  hearts
and minds of others with my few and feeble efforts.

I thank you for reminding me of my own human
  frailty,
even as I rage against the weakness and pain
  which entraps me so,
for I am but human and still in need of understanding;
but you have shown me the way, through my pain
  and yours, to understand the pain of others.

May I continue to walk this path humbly,
  prayerfully, soulfully, till my journey
  ends in You.

Amen